Relinking Life and Work

Rapoport et al.

Toward a Better Future

Starting in the early 1990s, many companies began embracing a range of innovative policies and programs to address the issue of integrating work and family life. These efforts marked an important first step in helping employees—particularly mothers of young children—accommodate their responsibilities to home and family. Nevertheless, often a large gap existed between the promise of such policies and programs and their implementation in practice. More and more, researchers, employers, and employees came to recognize that work-family benefits alone could not bring about the changes they hoped for.

It became clear that, instead of focusing on discrete work-family programs and policies, it was critical to look at the assumptions underlying how work is done in the organization, including the work cultures and structures. Extensive conversations with experts in the work-family field and with executives of companies that have comprehensive work-family policies have revealed possible new approaches to systemic change.

The projects described in this volume began as an experiment with a collaborative action research approach—one in which researchers work jointly with companies to bring about change that would facilitate work-family integration. At the time, though, it was impossible to articulate how the processes would unfold or what the outcomes would be. We were seeking to support companies that wanted to examine and were willing to try to change the work culture and the organization of work. Still, no one was confident this could be done without negative consequences to the bottom line. What was known, however, was that work-family issues make it difficult for many companies—even those with model work-family policies and generous benefits—to retain certain groups of women. Thus, these corporations wanted to address the issues of work-family integration and gender equity.

The companies' interest in work and family issues must be related to the bottom line in addition to broader goals. Only in this way can every individual—female or male—pursue her or his talents fully; can tomorrow's generation of children be well cared for by fathers as well as mothers; and can women and men contribute to their families and communities as well as to their work.

Major organizational change takes somewhere between eight and ten years. Thus, this study is not—and is not intended to be—a finished product. Rather, it is meant to stimulate employees and organizations to think differently and creatively about work structures and practices and to provide a framework for embracing change that benefits both companies and employees. And it suggests a productive methodology for achieving those goals.

Pegasus Communications, Inc. (tel) 781-398-9700 (fax) 781-894-7175

Despite the breadth and variety of these projects, many important issues have yet to be explored. This volume focuses primarily on the systemic changes in the workplace to advance gender equity and the integration of work and family life. Changes in the workplace and in gender roles also may spawn new ways of sharing family caregiving and participating in community activities. The integration of individuals, work, personal and family life, and community involvement in new and different configurations remains a challenge for the future.

—June H. Zeitlin
Director, Governance and Civil Society, Peace and Social Justice Program, Ford Foundation

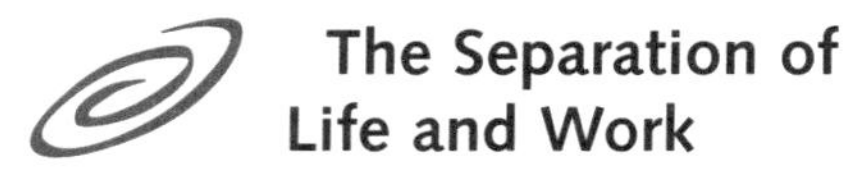

The Separation of Life and Work

Since the Industrial Revolution, American society—its workplaces, schools, families, and communities—has been organized as if only men go to work and only women stay at home. This division of labor brought with it the sense that work and family were necessarily distinct, a view that has never coincided with the reality of most people's lives. In practice, family and work have never been strictly separated.

Now, with more and more women in the labor market and more men doing slightly more in families, the strict separation of work and family is even less reflective of reality. And businesses are beginning to respond. Whereas employees' private lives were formerly "off the screen," more and more these concerns are addressed by special policies designed to help individuals juggle work and family and personal needs. What has not really changed, however, is the underlying conception that work and private life are separate and inherently adversarial.

Since the Industrial Revolution, American society has been organized as if only men go to work and only women stay at home.

The Strategic Linking of Work and Family

In the following pages, we examine the workplace and the family as integrated spheres. We reframe work-family issues as embedded in corporate culture and work practices, which therefore require systemic solutions rather than individual accommodations.

We also take a broad, inclusive view of what we mean by "family." Instead of using the word to mean immediate kin—spouse and children—we intend it to stand for all aspects of an individual's personal life: those involvements and commitments, both at home and in the community, that an individual has outside his or her employment.

Wanted: Employees Without a Life

We knew when we started this project that the modern workplace is far less than ideal for workers who want integrated lives. As one engineer put it, "The problem isn't for those who have decided to put work first and family second. They can do just fine here. And it isn't for those who have decided to put family first. They don't go far here but that's okay because that's what they've decided is important. The problem is for people like me who want both—a good family [life] and a good career."

The struggle to have both a good personal life and a good career arises from a dominant societal image of the ideal worker as "career-primary," the person who is able and willing to put work first, and for whom work time is infinitely expandable. We found that this view translates into work practices that include dawn meetings; planning sessions that run into the evening, often ending with the suggestion to "continue this over dinner"; and training programs requiring long absences from home. Commitment is measured by what one manager proudly declared as his definition of a star engineer: "someone who doesn't know enough to go home at night." At lower levels in the organization, the belief in the dominance of work translates into tight controls over worker time and flexibility.

In situations where "ideal workers" are assumed to be those whose first allegiance is to the job, people with career aspirations go to great lengths to keep personal issues from intruding into work. Some people give false reasons for leaving work early: They feel that attending a community board or civic meeting is not likely to brand them as uncommitted, while taking a child for a physical might. Some secretly take children on business trips. Others leave their computers on while picking up children from sporting events, hoping that colleagues passing by will think they are in a meeting.

Pegasus Communications, Inc. (tel) 781-398-9700 (fax) 781-894-7175

While both men and women in such environments have trouble juggling work and family, their experiences differ dramatically because of gender roles and societal expectations. For example, requests for flexibility have few career implications for those—typically men—whose family needs are short-term, such as the first few days after the birth of a child or the temporary illness of a son or daughter. But significant career consequences face those—mainly women—who have continuing family responsibilities, especially in environments that put a premium on perfect attendance and hours spent in the office. Caregivers who try to negotiate ongoing flexible arrangements run a great risk of being branded as less committed or less dependable. This is so even though many personnel manuals describe flexible options as readily available to all.

Women in corporations face an additional burden: Expectations that they are or should be "family-primary" tend to taint them as unfit for organizational life. As a result, some women—especially those in professional or managerial roles—feel they have to hide their families altogether. So while men keep family pictures on their desks and are congratulated for occasionally being late to early meetings because of family duties, women of equal stature feel pressure to keep their families off the organizational screen—a phenomenon one woman described as "operating under the radar." Indeed, one compliment often paid to top women is that "you'd never even know she had a child."

One manager defined a star engineer as "someone who doesn't know enough to go home at night."

Although it is no longer politically correct to suggest that women belong in the home and men belong at work, we found that these attitudes and beliefs still influence work practices. One male senior sales representative spoke for many when he explained: "The problem is greed. What I see is that younger families expect a lavish lifestyle and that means that wives have to work and so we here at the company are trying to accommodate that, and don't get me wrong, I think we should. But on the other hand, it's not really our fault."

The belief that society works best when women stay at home and men go to work creates real problems for people who step out of prescribed gender roles. Women who focus primarily on work, for example, often suffer negative career consequences. In explaining why one woman had failed a management review, one divisional manager said, "She probably thought it would be seen as positive that she was willing to sacrifice her family for work. But she has gone through two divorces and who knows who is taking care of those kids . . . that's not the kind of person we admire." These women are caught in a classic double bind: The work culture mandates that they subordinate caring for their families but punishes them for doing so.

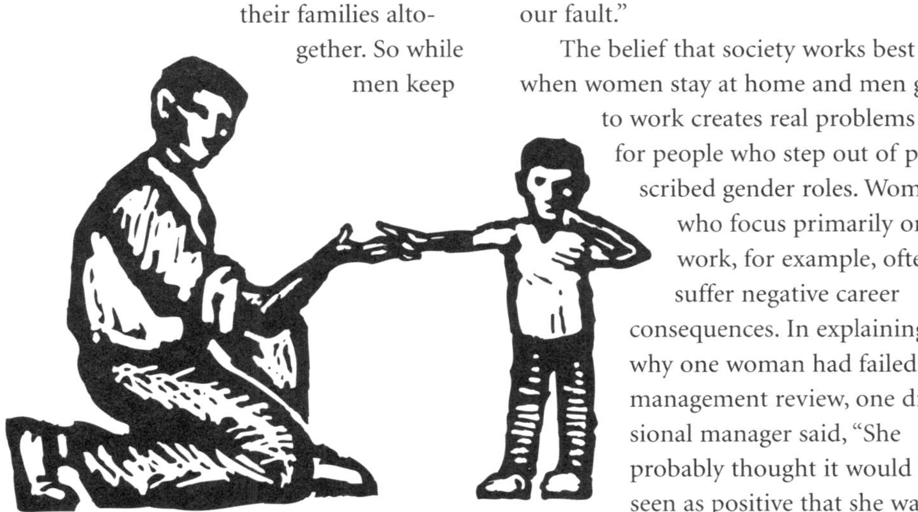

At the same time, men who want to share more of the responsibilities—and joys—of the private sphere face significant organizational constraints. Although they can achieve near-hero status for taking on some short-term family responsibilities, such as staying home to care for an infant with a fever, it is still extremely difficult for men to use "family-friendly" policies for any long-term arrangements. Many managers simply do not believe that men need flexibility for any extended period. A number of men told us they do not even try to plead their case because, in reality, flexible arrangements are available only to women. As one technical supervisor noted, "Men here are seen as wimps by senior management if they talk about their desire to spend time with their families."

Thus, the cultural separation of work and family by gender unfairly hinders women in the workplace while purporting to support them. At the same time, the narrow organizational definition of what constitutes a work-family need fails to legitimate men's concerns while maintaining the myth of their ideal worker status. The inequity is in the way work-family accommodations are tied to gender even though, on

Pegasus Communications, Inc. (tel) 781-398-9700 (fax) 781-894-7175

paper at least, work-family benefits are available to all.

Although both men and women spoke poignantly about the pain and unfairness of being forced to choose between work and family, we found that most people do not challenge the gender roles that encourage men to put careers first and women to focus first on family. These roles tend to be internalized at very deep, often unconscious levels. One successful young man said he wished to spend more time with his young children but feared that to be a good provider he had to make the same, work-driven choices his father did. And one young woman who had just passed up a promotion remarked how "unreasonable" it was of her to even think of taking the job. As she put it, "I couldn't possibly do that job and stay sane. I chose to have these kids, and now I have to take care of them."

Some workers are able, at times, to forge satisfactory links between work and family. The rest simmer with discontent.

When Individuals Try to Change

Some workers, because of their positions, their financial resources, or their perceived value as employees, are themselves able, at times, to forge satisfactory links between work and family. The rest simmer with discontent. In all cases, energy and loyalty are diverted unnecessarily from the organization. Because people feel powerless to deal with these concerns on their own, relevant work-related issues cannot be discussed at the collective level, where real systemic change might yield significant business and personal results.

When individuals change, but the system remains the same, there may be unexpected negative consequences for both. For example, one team leader we observed had arranged a four-day schedule to cut down on a long commute and to spend more time with her children. Not only did this arrangement serve her needs, but because the team leader rotated group members to take her place on the fifth day, she developed their self-management skills. By all measures, including productivity and satisfaction, the group was thriving. But the arrangement did not last long. In the end, the manager was stripped of her supervisory duties and moved to the bottom category of performance. Management regarded the team leader's efforts as a negative reflection of her future potential and management capability.

Similarly, a full-time sales technician who negotiated earlier hours was forced to give up the arrangement because her managers were unwilling to adjust their daily demands to conform to the schedule they had approved. From the beginning, the managers imposed so many "exceptions" that the employee was putting in extra hours and was unable to pick up her child at school much of the time—the reason she wanted the earlier hours in the first place. In the end, she reverted to her old schedule and became very disillusioned.

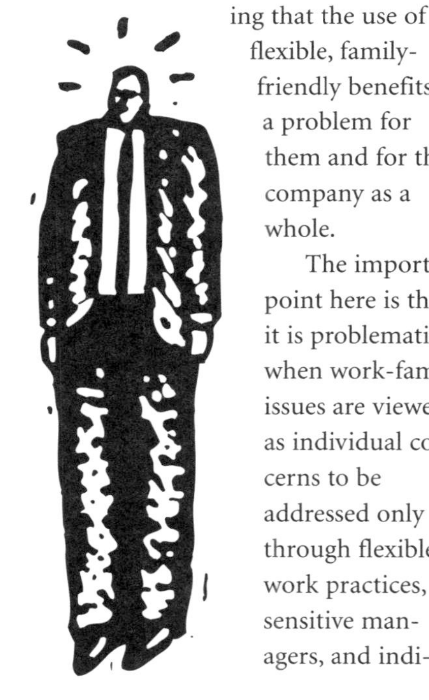

In this context, it is not surprising that managers typically view requests for flexibility as risky to grant. Even though they may sympathize and want to grant such requests, especially when it comes to their most valued employees, they worry about the potential negative consequences of allowing such arrangements. Not only do they worry that productivity might suffer, but they fear that, in negotiating and monitoring these special arrangements, they might have an increased workload. In addition, it is commonly felt that "merit-based" accommodations risk opening the flood gates and triggering similar requests from less "worthy" employees—which, if they are not granted, might lead to backlash and charges of favoritism. As a result, managers often end up sending negative signals indicating that the use of flexible, family-friendly benefits is a problem for them and for the company as a whole.

The important point here is that it is problematic when work-family issues are viewed as individual concerns to be addressed only through flexible work practices, sensitive managers, and indi-

Pegasus Communications, Inc. (tel) 781-398-9700 (fax) 781-894-7175

vidual accommodations. This approach often fails the individuals involved, and it may lead to negative career repercussions. More important, by viewing these issues as problems, companies miss opportunities for creative change.

For example, management could have perceived the unusual arrangement of the team leader with the four-day schedule as a chance to embrace this innovative work practice and to rethink the criteria for effective management. Similarly, the revised schedule of the sales technician could have been an opportunity to rethink the way time is used in the organization.

Consider, also, the following example: Two workers, one in sales and one in management, requested a job-sharing arrangement that would have allowed each of them to spend more time with their families. In an extensive proposal, they outlined how they would meet business needs under the new arrangement. As an added benefit, they also suggested a way to revamp the management development process so that a sales representative, working under the guidance of a sales manager, took on limited management duties. Such an apprenticeship model promised to be a significant improvement over the existing practice of "throwing sales people into management" with little training. Nevertheless, the company rejected the proposal because it was seen as stemming from a private concern (a desire for more personal time) rather than a work concern (a wish to increase the organization's effectiveness), and the opportunity was missed.

Despite these potential benefits to the company, we found that making the link between work and employees' personal lives in today's business environment is, to say the least, not easy. Significant organizational barriers—for example, assumptions about what makes a good worker, how productivity is achieved, and how rewards are distributed—militate against such linkage. At each of the companies we studied, we found that work-family benefits are designed and administered by the human resource function but implemented by line managers. Associating strategic initiatives with line managers and work-family concerns with human resources reinforces perceptions that business issues are separate, conceptually and functionally, from individuals' personal lives.

Putting Work-Family Issues on the Table

Putting work-family concerns on the table as legitimate issues for discussion in the workplace turns out to be liberating. By talking about such issues on an individual level in interviews and collectively during roundtables and group feedback, people realize that they are not alone in struggling to meet work and family/personal demands. Such discussions help people see that the problems are not solely of their own making, but stem from the way work is done today. The process of transforming personal issues to the collective level engages people's interest and leads to more creative ways of thinking. It also provides a strategic business opportunity that, if exploited correctly, can lead to improved bottom-line results.

For example, at one of our sites we documented the work practices of "integrated" individuals—people who link the two spheres of their life in the way they work. We found that integrated individuals draw not only on skills, competencies, and behaviors typical of the public, work sphere, such as rationality, linear thinking, assertiveness, and competition, but also on those associated with the private, personal sphere, such as collaboration, sharing, empathy, and nurturing. Their work practices include working behind the scenes to smooth difficulties between people that might disrupt the project, going out of their way to pass on key information to other groups, taking the time from their individual work to teach someone a new way of doing something, building on rather than attacking others' ideas in meetings, and routinely affirming and acknowledging the contributions of others. We showed the value-added nature of this work—the way it prevented problems, enhanced organizational learning, and encouraged collaboration—and created a vocabulary to talk about it and the relational skills it required. We called such people "lead users" and referred to their way of working as "relational practice." Offering a new vision of the ideal worker as an integrated individual, someone who brings skills to the job from both spheres of life, helps the organization recognize the importance of hiring and retaining such individuals.

THE SYNERGY OF LINKING WORK AND FAMILY

In addition to challenging employees to think differently about the way they work, we collaborated with work groups to reorganize and restructure the work process itself. The intervention described below shows how our project reframed perceptions about the connections between work and family and helped people see that legitimizing employees' personal issues presents unique opportunities for workplace innovations that enhance bottom-line business results.

This example comes from an engineering product development team, consisting primarily of men but including some women. Because managers at this site were good at granting flexibility for occasional emergency needs, most of the employees did not discuss or overtly recognize work-family issues as a problem. However, the long hours they felt compelled to work made their lives difficult. Here we found that addressing these personal issues helped uncover cultural assumptions and work structures that also interfered with an expressed business goal: shortening time to market.

At this site, we found that the team operated in a continual crisis mode that created enormous stress in the workplace and interfered with the group's efforts to improve quality and efficiency. This was an obvious problem for integrating work and personal life. One person, for example, said that she loved her job but that the demands ultimately made her feel like a "bad person" because they prevented her from "giving back to the community" as much as she desired.

By looking at the work environment in terms of work-family issues, we found that the source of the problem was a work culture that rewarded long hours on the job and measured employees' commitment by their continuous willingness to give work their highest priority. It also prized individual, "high-visibility" problem solving over less visible, everyday problem prevention.

Our interventions challenged these work culture norms. We also questioned the way time was allocated. Jointly, we structured work days to include blocks of uninterrupted "quiet time" during which employees could focus their attention on meeting their own objectives. This helped employees differentiate between unnecessary interruptions and interactions that are essential for learning and coordination. And the managers stopped watching continuously over their engineers, permitting more time for planning and problem prevention rather than crisis management. The result, despite contrary expectations, was an on-time launch of the new product and a number of excellence awards.

We used these data about relational practice to challenge the ways corporations value men and women and assess their prospects for advancement. For example, we indicated to one management team that by selecting as "top performers" only those—mostly men—who had public-sphere skills, they were inadvertently undermining the kinds of skills and team-oriented workers that their corporate mission statement professed to need. And with the manager who criticized the female employee for sacrificing family for her career, we suggested that it is the organizational definition of commitment and the image of the "ideal worker" that is the problem. Expecting an employee undergoing a management review to represent herself as "integrated"—when "separated" or "career-primary" is what is most valued—is unrealistic.

Where appropriate, we also pointed out to management the dissonance between policy and practice. For example, at an administrative site, despite the presence of a wide range of work-family policies, managers limited their use to very minor changes in daily work times. Employees dealt with the situation by "jiggling the system" on an ad hoc, individual basis to achieve the flexibility they needed, often by using sick days or vacation time. Thus, for instance, a man whose mother was chronically ill had to take a combination of ad hoc sick days and vacation days to be with her. The costs to the site for this companywide behavior were considerable in terms of unplanned absences, lack of coverage, turnover, and backlash against people who took the time they needed. It also created employee mistrust of an organization that claimed it had benefits but made using them so difficult that the

Pegasus Communications, Inc. (tel) 781-398-9700 (fax) 781-894-7175

result was lower morale and widespread cynicism.

By bringing family to bear on work, we also focused attention on the process by which work is accomplished. In one sales environment, for example, we found that a sales team habitually worked around the clock to complete proposals for prospective customers. In the morning, the workers were rewarded with cheers from managers and coworkers, complimenting them on their commitment and willingness to get the job done. In response to our interventions, one manager recognized that this behavior reflected poor work habits and made it tough on these people's family lives. Not only were their families suffering, but it took several days for these workers to recover, during which time they were less productive.

The manager told his team that he was disappointed in their behavior, that it demonstrated an inability to plan. He also began to share his perceptions with other managers. As a result, the sales team began to recognize and reward new work habits such as planning ahead and anticipating problems rather than waiting until they were crises.

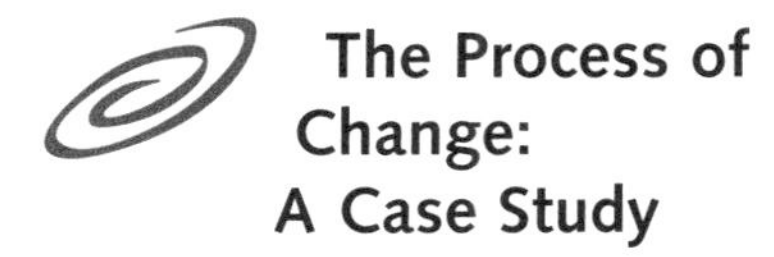

The Process of Change: A Case Study

Making significant changes in the workplace to help employees better integrate their work and personal lives requires an intensive method that actively engages the way people think and act. We call this method collaborative interactive action research. Unlike more traditional forms of research or consulting, our method is aimed at both increasing knowledge and effecting change. Research and intervention are intertwined. The process is one of mutual inquiry with our partners at the sites. It is not only we who are learning something about how the system works or introducing changes; nor is it only we who have the expertise and make the recommendations. These are all shared with our partners.

We illustrate the key tenets of our research method by presenting a case study below of the changes at one specific site: a large sales and service district of the Xerox Corporation. We highlight how looking at work through a work-family lens can clarify ways to deal with critical business issues. And we show how, by doing this, employers can promote the dual agenda of benefiting the business while addressing employees' concerns.

What we want to illuminate is not so much the particular changes brought about at the site, but the process of ongoing inquiry that connects work to family and community, links work-family issues to the way work is accomplished, and does so in a manner that is equitable for both men and women.

An Overview of Our Approach

Our research method has three key aspects. We start out by looking at work practices through a work-family lens. When we speak of using a "work-family lens," we mean engaging people in a process of reflection on aspects of the work that make it difficult to integrate work and personal life. This process of reflection helps people make a link between individual experiences and systemic issues, such as how work is structured, how time is spent, and how employees demonstrate commitment and competence. Since this process is not usually undertaken in corporations, it is generally greeted with some astonishment and often with resistance. But it is the process of collaboratively engaging such resistance by respecting it and talking about it that often leads to insights about alternative ways of working.

This process of reflection helps people make a link between individual experiences and systemic issues.

Second, we seek to link what we have learned about the work culture and practices to a salient business need the particular group is facing. Making this link establishes a mutual agenda, connecting individual work-family needs with business goals in ways that can potentially benefit both.

Finally, we press for change throughout the process—during employee interviews, roundtable discussions, and in experimental interventions like the one highlighted on p. 6. And we challenge assumptions about "unchangeable" conditions while encouraging out-of-the-box thinking about work practices.

Site Background

At the time of our research, the sales and service district had approximately 600 employees. They worked in three main functions: sales, service, and administration. The sales organization, with roughly equal numbers of men and women, was organized to serve dif-

Pegasus Communications, Inc. (tel) 781-398-9700 (fax) 781-894-7175

ferent product lines and different types of customers. The service technicians, mostly men, were responsible for maintaining equipment in different geographic areas. Administrative workers, primarily female, processed orders and scheduled installations. A senior management team (four men and one woman), drawn from the three functions, jointly managed the district, although one of the sales managers acted as the team's senior manager.

On paper, at least, the district enjoyed a companywide work-family benefits program, with flextime, compressed work weeks, job sharing, and other provisions. But such provisions were rarely used. Some managers were willing, off the record, to make short-term, informal accommodations for people who needed them. These workers, with few exceptions, were women in administration who were granted slight variations in their daily schedules, or what amounted to a limited form of flextime. While work-family issues were rarely, if ever, talked about openly in the district, they simmered under the surface and were frequently the topic of informal discussions.

Looking at Work Through a Work-Family Lens

We started our research at this site by interviewing more than 60 men and women at all levels across the three functions. To the surprise of respondents, and the active resistance of some, we focused not only on work-family issues, but more broadly on their ability to do what needed to be done on the job and still have time and energy for outside interests. In time, however, even resistant respondents shared their experiences with us.

Work-family concerns cut across the work force, occupying men as well as women, managers as well as frontline employees.

In general, talking with employees and managers about the boundary between work and personal concerns was often an emotional experience. People spoke about the stress in their families and how that affected their work. One sales manager, who had had the highest employee satisfaction ratings the prior year, talked about how devastating his divorce had been and how he worried now that his ratings were below par. Others took the opportunity to tell us that the work-family problem was merely one of women's greed for an elevated lifestyle.

These interviews and, indeed, the entire data collection process offered us opportunities to engage and challenge people's assumptions about the roles of men and women and the unspoken rules of the workplace. For example, we discussed other reasons besides "greed" why mothers might work and provided alternative scenarios for managers to think through some of their fears about workday flexibility.

As part of our data collection, we also conducted an employee survey, in part to help legitimize the issue in the eyes of a new senior management team. The survey confirmed our initial findings that work-family concerns cut across the work force, occupying men as well as women, managers as well as frontline employees.

Applying the Findings to a Critical Business Need

While we were talking with people about work and family, we were also learning about the significant business issues engaging the district. A recent customer survey, for example, revealed that customer relations were deteriorating and that improving these relationships could boost revenues. To address these findings, the district had adopted a new strategy of selling systems solutions. This strategy required close partnering with customers to jointly diagnose their needs and to create solutions to address them. It also had internal consequences, requiring a high degree of collaboration and coordination among the various functions.

When we looked at these issues through a work-family lens, we found that this strategy of customer focus, supported by internal coordination, was being undercut by the same work practices that made it tough for employees to integrate work and personal concerns. The district was supposed to be managed by a partnership, but each function had its own reward and reporting system, which tended to promote individual departments' goals over those of the district. Sales targets were increased every year without consulting the field. Service technicians increasingly were called upon to provide 24-hour service with a two-hour response time, and beepers meant that new calls came in while old problems were still being addressed. The culture was competitive and stressful.

Communication was another problem. Information was tightly held and finger-pointing was common. The service technicians did not know when to expect installations, and they blamed the sales reps for inflating estimates, which wreaked havoc with their own schedules. The sales representatives, in turn, blamed the service technicians for creating poor customer relations, which made their jobs harder, and blamed the administrative staff for not getting their paychecks out on time. The administrative staff, meantime, blamed both sales and service for being slow to provide the information they needed to schedule orders and deliveries.

We captured these connections between business issues and work-family concerns in our diagnosis—the "mirror" we held up. Cross-functional collaboration was not a reality at the district, with negative consequences for the business and employees. Groups worked at cross-purposes and customers suffered. The individualistic culture also meant that people were reluctant to help each other out, either at work or in meeting other responsibilities. As a result, everybody's work took more time, and employees were left on their own to attend to personal concerns.

Pressing for Change

While management could relate our findings to their business, they were skeptical about the connection between the structure and culture of work and employees' work and family concerns. They were even more resistant to the specific proposal we made: to establish a group to sell, service, and support one significant customer—what we called a "customer slice." Such a group, we thought, could be a pilot to develop broader collaboration and show the benefits of cooperation. This kind of collaboration, we believed, would make work more predictable and less stressful.

These benefits would spill over into the family arena; the same kind of cooperation around work would translate into support and flexibility regarding family. People would cover for each other and take family issues into account in planning work.

Management requested that we present the "customer slice" concept to employee roundtables. At first, employees were bewildered by the idea. The prevailing response was, "We are all separate groups who do our own work. There is no overlap." But as they talked about their experiences, they discovered that they were not as separate as they thought. Sales reps complained about the lack of coverage for their accounts when they were out on vacation or had family emergencies. Service technicians felt that they were always in a reactive mode, making it very difficult to take control of either their work or their private lives. And administrative workers felt they were being treated as scapegoats for breakdowns in the system that occurred because other functions failed to provide them with the information they needed to process orders and do their work. To their surprise, roundtable members concluded that a multifunctional group might make their work easier and help them gain control over their lives.

Management remained skeptical. But by collaboratively engaging their resistance, we emerged with the possibility of using the Offset Group (a fictitious name) as a pilot for the project. A product group, it met our critical requirements: Sales, service, and administration shared a common set of customers. From management's perspective the Offset Group was low risk: Originally a separate company that had never been fully integrated into the district, it had performed below expectation and had suffered poor customer service ratings for years.

Changes in the Offset Group. In collaboration with senior management, we began the change process with a core team of managers and decided to involve the entire 75-person Offset Group later. The core group consisted

Pegasus Communications, Inc. (tel) 781-398-9700 (fax) 781-894-7175

of three managers from service, two from sales, and one from administration. But over the nine-month period of our involvement, the group brought in other people with ties to the same product. The group's accomplishments were considerable: Sales exceeded targets, customer satisfaction improved, and group members reported feeling more supported, more in control of their work and work-family issues, and less stressed.

Customer satisfaction improved, and group members reported feeling more supported, more in control of their work and work-family issues, and less stressed.

These successes had their roots in the first meeting of the Offset Group. Initially, the group members could see no reason to have another meeting with each other; they were already stretched getting their own work done. We and the project manager urged the employees to talk about their work to see if a reason for working together would emerge—and it did. One of the service managers mentioned that he was about to lose four experienced service technicians at the end of the month in the first voluntary reduction in force. The sales managers were alarmed; not only were they unaware of this development but they also feared it would have a negative impact on their ability to sell and install equipment.

With this initial recognition of interdependence, the group members became more committed to the idea that a multifunctional group could benefit everybody. They agreed to meet again in three weeks and, for the next nine months, scheduled monthly meetings. At subsequent meetings, the group continued to find areas of business collaboration. They developed a strategy for their project and studied the connections among the business functions at a time when the district was undergoing significant downsizing and restructuring. An early success kept the group going: One service manager was able to save a major sale to a large customer who was frustrated by the poor performance of older equipment. Even though the service manager received no official credit for the sale, it helped service because, after that, sales managers began to share actual sales data instead of projections. As a result, service could plan scheduled maintenance and have a qualified team ready to handle installations. The group also addressed other problems, such as how to improve the flow of paperwork and how to accommodate higher installation demands with downsizing and limitations on overtime.

As the group became more cohesive, discussions of work-family issues became more legitimate. In fact, on one occasion when a senior manager was present, the group asked to keep the meeting as "theirs" alone, so they could "talk about personal things here." Members also brought to the group specific problems they wanted to address. For example, we worked with sales managers to consider how part-time work could be managed and with service managers to benchmark alternative work schedules.

The Benefits of Collaboration. The advantages of the project went beyond the Offset Group. Employees in the district began to appreciate the close connection between business issues and work-family concerns and began to feel safer about proposing new approaches. The service groups, for instance, developed a scheduling system where employees could trade weekend work for days off during the week to cope with staff cuts and more 24-hour call contracts.

In the sales function, an employee task force, with senior management's endorsement, moved back the starting times for all morning meetings and ended afternoon meetings earlier to take into account employees' work-family commitments. And a longstanding, controversial proposal for an alternative schedule in sales was now approved.

Throughout the nine-month pilot project, we saw our role as supporting the group's effort, inserting the dual agenda whenever possible, and being there as needed. We attended almost every meeting and frequently interviewed members individually. We helped the group track its progress by analyzing and reporting back the many opportunities it had created for collaboration. At the end of the nine months, a survey we administered showed that the group members felt they were working well together and had improved their ability to serve customers. On the work-family side, members reported feeling less stressed, more in control, and more supported.

Stepping Back

Despite such successes, keeping the dual agenda on the table turned out to be more difficult than we had anticipated. First, we decided it would help to "jump start" the team if they could find a business issue around which to organize. While this proved useful, it meant that the connection between work and work-family concerns was not always apparent. Second, we could have done more to keep the dual agenda in mind, such as interviewing team members and encouraging them to make connections between work and family—processes that had proved successful in the earlier phases of the work.

On the positive side, we maintained close ties to senior management throughout the process. This led to the formation of a sales task force that looked at barriers to work-family integration in the sales organization, such as early morning meetings and unstated requirements of "face time." We also met with the senior service manager to help address such specific problems as scheduling flextime and meeting customer needs. Other managers in the district were involved in innovative experiments of their own. We helped make these successes more visible by reporting them across functional and hierarchical boundaries.

Late in the process, we learned that the district had previously tried a cross-functional approach in this same product group, which failed. Senior managers wondered why the Offset Group was a success. A number of explanations are possible: a talented project manager, our operational support of the team, its early identification of one problem that could be resolved collaboratively, several quick successes.

Based on our experience, however, we believe that another, more important reason exists: The members of the group came to believe that the group would make a real difference to the company *and* give them more control over their lives at work and at home. This connection to their personal lives engaged their creativity and energized them to make the group successful.

Lessons and Challenges

Our work taught us much about the process of linking work and family that other organizations can now adapt. In essence, our experience shows that changes in work practices can be brought about by looking at work through a work-family lens, linking what is learned from that process to a salient business need, and pushing for change at each step of the process.

We begin to make the systemic link between work practice and work-family integration by engaging three lines of questioning:

- How does work get done around here?
- What are the employees' personal stories of work-family integration?
- What is it about the way work gets done around here that makes it difficult (or easy) to integrate work and personal life so that neither one suffers?

Ultimately, however, the success of our method also depends on the existence of two specific conditions:

- a safe environment that minimizes individual risk, freeing employees to take part in the change; and
- room in the process for engaging people's resistance—in other words, addressing their objections, concerns, and underlying feelings with a view toward creating options that were not previously envisioned.

Creating Safety and Minimizing Risk

By giving people permission to talk about their feelings and their personal dilemmas in the context of redesigning work, a surprising level of energy, creativity, and innovative thinking gets released. But raising these issues may not be easy for those who fear they will be branded as less committed or undependable if they acknowledge such difficulties. At the same time, managers who are used to viewing gains for the family as productivity losses for the business may fear they will bear all the risks of innovation.

Therefore, collaboration and sharing the risks across the organization are important aspects of the process. In concrete terms, this means getting some sign from senior managers that they are willing to suspend, if only temporarily, some of the standard operating procedures that the work groups have identified as barriers both to work-family integration and productivity. Such a signal from upper management also helps people believe that cultural change is possible and provides higher-level support to individual managers seeking to bring about change.

At our sites, these signs took different forms. One site suspended work rules that narrowly defined how cus-

Pegasus Communications, Inc. (tel) 781-398-9700 (fax) 781-894-7175

tomer needs can be met, while another granted a grace period to accommodate possible short-term losses in productivity arising from the change process. The point is that for our method to work, employees need concrete evidence that they are truly able to control some of the conditions that affect their own productivity. And managers need assurance that they will not be penalized for experimenting in this fashion.

Engaging Resistance

The process of relinking work to family creates resistance because it touches core beliefs about society, success, gender roles, and the place of work and family in our lives. We found, however, that such resistance—both within the organization and among research team members—almost always points to something important that needs to be acknowledged and addressed collaboratively. Engaging with this type of resistance means listening to and learning from people's objections, incorporating their concerns and new ideas, and working together to establish a dual agenda.

The process of relinking work to family creates resistance because it touches core beliefs about society, success, gender roles, and the place of work and family in our lives.

Resistance surfaced around a number of issues. Offering collaboration in place of "expert advice," for example, was often met with frustration. At the same time, people continually asked us, during interviews, roundtables, and feedback sessions, what work-family integration had to do with work. And they challenged the notion that changing the way work gets done could also benefit employees in their personal lives. Research team members exhibited resistance by attempting to shorten the process. They often told people what to do or resisted collaborative discussion about their own limitations. But to be effective, the process cannot be shortchanged. It requires trust, openness, and a willingness to learn from others.

Our position as outsiders allowed us to help reframe old ways of thinking, and to shift the discussion from what is, to what could be. Collabora-tion was necessary to allay fears and to engage the resistance associated with examining the assumptions underlying proposed changes.

Challenges

Our method has produced notable operational successes that have continued beyond the experimental phase of the interventions. The next challenge is how to sustain these efforts over the long term and to diffuse them beyond the local sites. While we are still discovering ways to meet that challenge, we do know that lasting organizational change requires mutual learning by individuals, by the group, and by the system as a whole. We also know that it is important to continue to keep the double agenda on the table, ensuring that benefits from the change process continue to accrue to employees and their families as well as to the organization. If not, the individual energy that this method unleashes will dissipate—triggering anger and mistrust within the organization.

What's more, if local changes are to be sustained and if lessons from them are to be diffused, the work needs to be

CAN YOUR COMPANY BENEFIT FROM RELINKING?

How can you tell whether your company would benefit from steps to relink life and work? The signals can be detected in individual employees' behavior and attitudes, as well as in larger patterns of behavior within the organization overall. Below are some examples of key indicators that a company should explore issues concerning the connections between life and work:

Employee Indicators	Organizational Indicators
Complaints about overload	Loss of valued employees
Stress and fatigue	Reduced creativity
Sudden changes in performance	New initiatives that falter
Low morale	Decision-making paralysis
	Inefficient work practices: continuous crisis, excessive long hours, frequent emergency meetings

legitimized so that operational successes become widely known. Given the tendency to marginalize and individualize work-family issues, the overt support of senior management is essential here. Such support reinforces "work-family" as a business issue that is owned by the corporation as a whole.

Lasting change also requires an infrastructure, a process for carrying the lessons learned and the methodology used to other parts of the organization. In one organization, that process took the form of an operations steering committee working hand-in-hand with the research team to carry on the work in other parts of the corporation.

Our experience also suggests that multiple points of diffusion must exist. We sought opportunities, for instance, to present our work as part of special events as well as operational reviews and to look for internal allies among line managers, people involved in organizational change, and so on. Diffusion is also a challenge because, as people reflect on how the various operational pilots meet business needs, they tend to want to pass on to other teams only the results that yielded the productivity gains, rather than information about the process itself. This tendency shortchanges the process and seriously undermines the chances for replicating its success and sustainability.

Relinking Work and Family Life

As corporations continue to restructure and reinvent themselves, our findings suggest that linking such change efforts to employees' personal concerns greatly enhances their chances for success. Such relinking energizes employees to participate fully in the process because there are personal benefits to be gained. It also uncovers hidden or ignored assumptions about work practices and organizational cultures that can undermine the changes envisioned.

But relinking work and family is not something that can be accomplished simply by wishing it were so or by pointing out the negative consequences of separation. It is something that touches the very core of our beliefs about society, success, and gender. And it implies rethinking the place of families and communities and a new look at how we can nurture and strengthen these vital building blocks of our society.

The assumed separation of the domestic and nondomestic spheres breeds inequality, since present practices, structures, and policies—at all levels of society—favor the economic sphere above all others. As a result, employment concerns are assumed to take precedence over other concerns; achievement in the employment sector is assumed to be the major source of self-esteem and the measure of personal success. And, since employment skills are most highly valued and compensated, they dominate government, educational, and organizational policy.

In the end, the goal of relinking work and family life is not simple and it is not just about being "whole." It is about shifting to a more equitable society in which family and community are valued as much as paid work is valued, and where men and women have equal opportunity to achieve in both spheres. As our work shows, such change is possible and provides real benefits not only to individuals and their families, but also to business and society.

Additional Resources

Lotte Bailyn, *Breaking the Mold: Women, Men and Time in the New Corporate World* (Free Press, 1993)

Arlie Hochschild, *The Second Shift: Working Parents and the Revolution at Home* (Avon Books, 1997)

Rosabeth Moss Kanter, *Work and Family in the United States* (Russell Sage Foundation, 1977)

Leslie Perlow, *Finding Time: How Corporations, Individuals, and Families Can Benefit from New Work Practices* (Cornell University Press, 1997)

Rhona Rapoport and Robert N. Rapoport, *Dual-Career Families Reexamined: New Integrations of Work and Family* (Harper Colophon, 1977)

Juliet Schor, *The Overworked American: The Unexpected Decline of Leisure* (Basic Books, 1993)

Principal Authors

Rhona Rapoport is codirector of the Institute of Family and Environmental Research in London, England. She coauthored the first publication on dual-career families and is the coauthor of several books, including *Dual Career Families Re-examined: New Integrations of Work and Family* (Harper Colophon, 1977); *Leisure and the Family Life Cycle* (Routledge and Kegan Paul, 1975); and *Men and Women as Equals at Work.* She is currently a consultant to the Ford Foundation and other organizations, working on gender equity and organizational change. She is also a founding partner of Lume International, LLP, a company dedicated to working with organizations to redesign work practices in line with a dual agenda: to help male and female employees integrate their work with their private lives and at the same time help companies more effectively to achieve their business goals.

Lotte Bailyn is the T Wilson (1953) Professor of Management at the MIT Sloan School of Management. She served as the Matina S. Horner Distinguished Visiting Professor at Radcliffe's Public Policy Institute for the period 1995–1997. Her latest book is *Breaking the Mold: Women, Men and Time in the New Corporate World* (Free Press, 1993). She is also a founding partner of Lume International, LLP.

Deborah Kolb is professor of management at the Simmons Graduate School of Management and director of the Simmons Institute on Leadership and Change. She is also a senior fellow at the Program on Negotiation, Harvard University, where she codirects the Negotiation in the Workplace Program, and is the author of several books on mediation and work. She is also a founding partner of Lume International, LLP.

Joyce K. Fletcher is an associate professor of cooperative education at Northeastern University and Asa S. Knowles Research Fellow at Northeastern's new Office for the Study of Work and Learning. Her Ph.D. dissertation, "Toward a Theory of Relational Practice in Organizations: A Feminist Reconstruction of Real Work," grew out of the research for this report, and will be published as a book by the MIT Press. She is also a founding partner of Lume International, LLP.

Pegasus Communications, Inc. (tel) 781-398-9700 (fax) 781-894-7175

Contributing Authors

Dana E. Friedman, cofounder and former copresident of the Families and Work Institute, designs national research studies, management training programs, employee needs assessments, and human resource strategic plans aimed at helping people balance their work and family lives. She is currently director of corporate solutions for the Resource Group, a division of Corporate Family Solutions, where she is senior vice president. She has been a senior research associate at The Conference Board and has worked at the Carnegie Corporation.

Barbara Miller, president of Artemis Management Consultants, has consulted to organizations such as Intel, AT&T, and Stanford University for the past 20 years. She has published numerous articles on management skills and has taught graduate courses in human resources and organizational development at the University of San Francisco.

Susan Eaton is a doctoral student at the MIT Sloan School of Management. She worked for 12 years as a negotiator, manager, and trainer at the Service Employees International Union, AFL-CIO. She has written and consulted on women in the work force, leadership development, and labor law.

Maureen Harvey is an organizational consultant with over 15 years of experience in the electronic technology field, and is a partner of Lume International LLP.

Additional Research Members

Xerox Corporation: Robin Johnson, University of Virginia; Leslie Perlow, University of Michigan Business School and author of *Finding Time: How Corporations, Individuals, and Families Can Benefit from New Work Practices* (Cornell University Press, 1997), which is based on this project.

Tandem Computers, Inc.: Jerry Garfield; Roy Jacques, California School of Professional Psychology; Amy Lyman, Great Place to Work Institute; Joyce Ortega; Erica Pelavin, California School of Professional Psychology; Suzanne Van Stralen

Corning, Inc.: Ellen Galinsky and James Levine, Families and Work Institute

This volume is an edited version of a report originally published by the Ford Foundation. It is based on a research project in collaboration with Xerox Corporation, Tandem Computers, Inc., and Corning, Inc.

Pegasus Communications, Inc. (tel) 781-398-9700 (fax) 781-894-7175

The Innovations in Management Series

The *Innovations in Management Series*, available through Pegasus Communications, Inc., features in-depth analyses of both leading-edge and foundational topics in systems thinking, organizational learning, and business management. Concise and comprehensive, these volumes are ideal for customizing your learning—whether your interest is in the tools of systems thinking, the disciplines of organizational learning, or the latest management ideas as expressed by the most prominent thinkers in the business world. Watch for upcoming new titles, and build your *Innovations in Management* library!

Topics on the Leading Edge

From Mechanistic to Social Systemic Thinking: A Digest of a Talk by Russell L. Ackoff, by Lauren Johnson

The Natural Step: A Framework for Achieving Sustainability in Our Organizations, by Karl-Henrik Robèrt

The Soul of Corporate Leadership: Guidelines for Values-Centered Governance, by William J. O'Brien

Systems Thinking Tools & Applications

Applying Systems Archetypes, by Daniel H. Kim and Colleen P. Lannon

Toward Learning Organizations: Integrating Total Quality Control and Systems Thinking, by Daniel H. Kim

Designing a Systems Thinking Intervention: A Strategy for Leveraging Change, by Michael Goodman, Richard Karash, Colleen Lannon, Kellie Wardman O'Reilly, and Don Seville

Systems Stories

Anxiety in the Workplace: Using Systems Thinking to Deepen Understanding, by Janet M. Gould, John J. Voyer, and David N. Ford

Facing the Competition: An Organization Mobilizes for Large-Scale Change, by Nagah Ramadan, Patrick Parker-Roach, and Carl Klempner

Special Topics

Creating Sustainable Organizations: Meeting the Ecological, Economic, and Social Challenges of the 21st Century, by Sara Schley and Joseph Laur

Relinking Life and Work: Toward a Better Future, by Rhona Rapoport, Lotte Bailyn, Joyce K. Fletcher, and Deborah Kolb

Topics & Tools in Organizational Learning

Creating Value: Linking the Interests of Customers, Employees, and Investors, by Paul O'Malley

To order any of the above volumes, or to learn about our *Innovations in Management Series* quantity discounts and standing order plan, feel free to phone us toll-free at 1-800-272-0945. Visit our Web site, too, at www.pegasuscom.com to read more about the titles in this series.

Also, if you enjoyed reading this volume and have an idea for the *Innovations in Management Series*, please feel free to contact us. We welcome your thoughts and invite you to put us in contact with other potential authors as well.

Lauren Johnson, Series Editor
(ljohnson@pegasuscom.com)

Kellie Wardman O'Reilly, Publications Director
(kellie@pegasuscom.com)

IMS010

Z0501
$1.95
An Educational Coloring Book of
STATE BIRDS
WEST MANCHESTER
COMMUNITY LIBRARY
76 N. Main Street
Manchester, N. H. 03102
SPIZZIRRI